The IIA Handbook Series

AUDITING VENDOR RELATIONSHIPS

By
Mark Salamasick, CIA, CISA, CSP, MBA
Chris Linsteadt, MBA, MS

**The Institute of
Internal Auditors**

Disclosure

The IIA publishes this document for informational and educational purposes. This document is intended to provide information, but is not a substitute for legal or accounting advice. The IIA does not provide such advice and makes no warranty as to any legal or accounting results through its publication of this document. When legal or accounting issues arise, professional assistance should be sought and retained.

The Professional Practices Framework for Internal Auditing (PPF) was designed by The IIA Board of Directors' Guidance Task Force to appropriately organize the full range of existing and developing practice guidance for the profession. Based on the definition of internal auditing, the PPF comprises *Ethics* and *Standards*, *Practice Advisories,* and *Development and Practice Aids,* and paves the way to world-class internal auditing.

This guidance fits into the Framework under the heading *Development and Practice Aids.*

ISBN 0-89413-511-2
03330   09 /03
First Printing

CONTENTS

ABOUT THE AUTHORS

Mark Salamasick, CIA, CISA, CSP, MBA, teaches Information Technology Risk Management and Internal Audit at The University of Texas at Dallas (UTD) along with providing audit and risk management consulting. During the fall of 2003, he is starting a new IIA Endorsed Internal Audit Program. He is a member of The Institute of Internal Auditor's (IIA's) International Board of Research Advisors, and serves on the Board of Governors of The IIA's North Chapter, the board of the UNT IIA Endorsed Program, and the Executive Advisory Board for the UTD Accounting Program.

Mr. Salamasick was Senior Vice President in the Internet/Intranet Services group for Bank of America for the past two years. For 18 years he was an Information Technology Audit Director at the bank. In those roles he dealt with many outsourced operations, along with the audit liaison to clients. Prior to working for the bank he was a Senior Consultant for Anderson Consulting in the Advanced Information Technology Group. He has taught full-time at the Central Michigan University and part-time for Northwood Institute. He worked on the development of an online audit course for the University of Maryland.

He received the 1994 IIA International Audit and Technology award for his efforts on the Systems Auditability and Control work related to Emerging Technology. He also participated in the update of the 2001/2002 eSAC modules for The IIA. He received his bachelor's and master's degrees from Central Michigan University with an emphasis in accounting and management. He can be reached at marksalamasick@yahoo.com.

Chris Linsteadt, MBA, MS, is currently an independent audit and risk management consultant. Previously, he was employed at the Federal Deposit Insurance Company (FDIC) as an Account Officer in Risk Management. His responsibilities at the FDIC related to identification and assessment of risks for the portfolio of assets held by the company. He was instrumental in helping to develop a nationwide computer database for the FDIC that managed all risk and insurance information. He has passed all parts of the CPA exam for Texas and holds a master's of science in accounting along with a master's of business administration He can be reached at ac120@comcast.net.

ACKNOWLEDGMENTS

We would like to thank The Institute of Internal Auditors for supporting this project. In particular we would like to thank Stacy Mantzaris, Assistant Vice President, Seminars Group, and Evy Acevedo, Coordinator, Educational Products. We would also like to thank Don Sparks, Assistant Vice President, Online Services Group, for providing us with the research information related to our survey. This information was extremely beneficial. We also appreciate the oversight and mentorship provided by Anna Nicodemus and the Educational Products Committee. Without their support, we could not have completed this Handbook.

Also, our gratitude is extended to the participants who attended the "Roundtable" session at The University of Texas at Dallas on October 25, 2002. Our two guest speakers, Jim Ramsey of PricewaterhouseCoopers and Mark Halliwell from Ernst & Young, provided valuable information on trends and best practices related to outsourced operations. The participants provided valuable insight and commentary for the development of this topic. We would also like to thank their various companies for allowing the participants the time to attend this session.

Those attending included the following:

John Calhoun
CEC Entertainment

Mark Halliwell
Ernst & Young

Renee Herrera
The University of Texas at Dallas

Eddie Holt
Texas Instruments

Anne Linsteadt
Dallas Nephrology Associates

Andrew Lupton
Bank of America

Dennis McGuffie
Triad Hospitals

Anna Nicodemus
EDS

Dr. Hasan Pirkul
The University of Texas at Dallas

Joan Bradford Pope
Independent CPA

Jim Ramsey
PricewaterhouseCoopers

Jodi Schmieg
EDS

Calvin J. Wilson
Nortel Networks

A special thanks goes to The University of Texas at Dallas for providing us with the space to conduct our forum, and to Dr. Hasan Pirkul, Dean, School of Management, for his introduction during the roundtable session.

Finally, we would both like to thank our wives, Terry Salamasick and Anne Linsteadt, for providing us with unbounded support and encouragement. We would also like to thank our children, Chris Salamasick and Allison and Luke Linsteadt, who put up with our many hours of work with very little complaint.

EXECUTIVE SUMMARY OUTSOURCED PROCESSES AND THE INTERNAL AUDITOR

Outsourcing: A partnership between a client and an outside vendor, both sharing a common vision to effectively, efficiently, and accurately accomplish an agreed-upon process for the benefit of both parties.

The current trend toward outsourcing is continuing today at a rapid pace. Processes are being turned over and control is being relinquished for many tasks that have been identified as non-core to the organization. Many times, these outsourcing partnerships are successful and result in increased profits for the organization. However, on some occasions, outsourcing can have unintended and unforeseen consequences for the bottom line of the organization. To avoid these unwanted risks, management should employ the full use of the internal auditing department and the skills that many of the staff members bring to the table. Unlike any other time in our history, internal audit has the opportunity to add value to critical business ventures for the organization. Instead of adopting the old role of identifying weaknesses after the fact and verifying the existence of controls, internal auditors have the opportunity to provide best practices for their management team and act as consultants, especially in the area of outsourcing. Management is wasting a valuable resource if they do not involve internal audit in the process of outsourcing from the moment it is considered all the way through to the monitoring process. As a research tool for this Handbook, a survey was implemented. One of the questions asked was, "Is internal audit involved in the creation of an outsourcing partnership?" Almost 72% of the respondents indicated that they were not involved. In this Handbook, we advocate for the auditors' involvement throughout the outsourcing processes. Our aim is to provide internal auditors with the tools necessary to create a successful partnership for outsourced services and to provide management with the assurance that the outsourced processes are effective and efficient.

One of the problems with outsourcing is the shift of the control environment to outside the organization. Although many companies are not comfortable with this shift, the very survival of some companies depends on quickly outsourcing business functions that are not core to the enterprise. This type of outsourcing has been called "right-sourcing." In right-sourcing, you have identified a process that is core to your survival in the marketplace and have realized that you do not have the expertise, capital, or personnel to conduct the process in-house. An example of this would be those who are just starting out and don't have the size or expertise to warrant performance of all functions. In other cases, functions like payroll and technology that require significant infrastructure may be best performed by a company with expertise in that area. Internal audit can assist in the identification and sourcing of the right business functions. An opportunity exists to leverage another organization that may have better expertise and leverage. With that expertise may come a mature control environment and ability to place reliance on the audit and control environment of the vendor. Identifying situations and categorizing them as an outsourcing or right-sourcing decision is one of the functions that internal audit should complete for management as a part of due diligence.

Whenever a company enters into an outsourcing arrangement, they have expanded and changed the control environment for the process. Auditors are in the best position and have the best tools to understand and manage the risks that flow from these relationships. In a true outsourcing situation, companies are giving up control of processes that can have varying impacts on the organization. Loss of control may lead to poor quality, a bad reputation in the marketplace, legal consequences, or a loss of profits; however, these same conditions can exist if the function is maintained in-house. One of the purposes of this Handbook is to point out the potential for value-added services by the internal audit staff in these situations. If internal audit is involved with the outsourcing arrangement from inception to monitoring, they can help to ensure the success of the partnership. If, however, outsourcing is entered into without proper consideration of the process and the associated risks, it can have devastating consequences. As this Handbook goes to press, vendors and partners of companies such as WorldCom, Enron, and Tyco are becoming all too familiar with these risks and the associated fallout that comes with selecting the wrong partner or process to outsource.

Throughout this Handbook we will see how the internal auditor can affect the process of outsourcing. As we found through our survey process, most auditors are only involved after the process has been completed and they are only responsible for auditing vendor performance against the contract. As Jim Ramsey from PricewaterhouseCoopers noted, "The public accounting firms are brought in after everything has gone wrong in the outsourcing relationship and asked to help fix it." We believe that a successful outsourcing arrangement should be a true partnership resulting in a win/win for the client and the service provider. This type of partnership can only be created if due diligence is completed on the part of the client. Due diligence includes the complete involvement of internal audit. The auditor has the chance to help management in its efforts to create a solid relationship with the vendor. Through the due diligence process, internal audit can ensure that key success factors are considered, such as communications, the impact of change on employees, strategic understanding of the business, the setting of clear expectations, gap analysis, feedback process, and many others. We will see throughout the Handbook that risk is always a part of outsourcing and, once again, internal audit will have the chance to assist management in the identification and mitigation of those risk factors in order to achieve a successful outsourcing partnership.

Outsourcing is a way of doing business effectively and the key factor is to ensure that you only outsource the appropriately identified business functions. In the following chapters, we will examine the need for this discussion, a brief history of outsourcing, the risk factors that are involved with outsourcing, techniques for dealing with the risk, a sample audit program for outsourced services, and the future of internal audit and outsourcing. We believe that outsourcing is a valuable business tool that can be made even more effective with the proper involvement of internal audit. The professionals that work in the internal auditing department bring with them a unique set of skills that allow them to assist with successful relationship building and risk management. Internal audit can help management better understand their needs and set the proper expectations for the process. Once those parameters have been established, creating an effective outsourcing partnership should be easier. Opportunities exist to leverage the expertise of the vendor internal auditor and have that additional independent resource evaluation of the control. The audit relationship between the organizations should be built on mutual trust, just like other parts of the outsource relationship.

The chapters are outlined as follows:

Chapter 1 takes a look at the history and the progression of outsourcing. In this chapter we examine some of the reasons behind the need to outsource and begin to lay a foundation for more due diligence in the outsourcing area.

Chapter 2 examines the requirements for a successful marriage — what it takes to have a terrific outsourcing partnership.

Chapter 3 takes a look at the issues and control objectives that surround outsourcing. We examine management's goals as they pertain to outsourcing and begin to look at some of the issues that are unique to the outsourcing process.

Chapter 4 identifies the risks that are associated with outsourcing. Many risks arise when a process is turned over to a vendor; we attempt to identify and list them in order of significance.

Chapter 5 discusses risk management. In this chapter we lay a framework for methods and techniques that can be used when dealing with risk.

Chapter 6 presents the audit program. We take you on a step-by-step plan for assuring your vendor relations. The audit program presented in this chapter represents a risk-based approach to auditing vendor relationships with particular emphasis on planning and setting objectives. This chapter assists the auditor by identifying risks associated with outsourcing and recognizing the various consequences that can flow from those risks.

Chapter 7 presents the reader with our vision of the future as it relates to outsourcing. Where do we go from here? What will be the role of the internal auditor? These and other issues are addressed in the final chapter.

Appendix A: Case examples, with discussions about outsourcing from companies and organizations such as National Geographic, First Energy Corporation, and Hughes Supply. Top audit executives discuss their experiences and concerns with outsourcing. The companies describe some of the biggest risks they face from outsourcing and some of the techniques that they use to mitigate those risks.

Appendix B: A presentation and analysis of the online survey that was conducted for the preparation of this Handbook.

FOREWORD
METHODOLOGY

This Handbook was completed with research material provided by an online questionnaire supported by the Global Auditing Information Network (GAIN), a database supported by The Institute of Internal Auditors (IIA), and a "Roundtable Discussion" hosted by The IIA and The University of Texas at Dallas. The questionnaire and the roundtable both provided valuable insight from audit and business professionals regarding vendor relationships.

The online questionnaire asked a series of questions that were aimed at determining how much involvement the internal audit department had in establishing outsourced or vendor relations. The questions also asked about frequency and types of audit programs companies had in place to assure their vendor relations. We were also curious to know at what stage the internal audit department became involved with the assurance of outsourced partners or the outsourced process. As we mention throughout the book, we discovered that internal audit is rarely involved in the beginning stages of outsourcing. The trend is that auditors are called in once the outsource agreement starts to have problems. Auditors have the knowledge and risk management tools necessary to help alleviate common outsourcing problems if they are allowed to have input during the entire outsourcing cycle. We believe the auditors should be involved at all points, including:

- The need analysis for outsourcing:

    - Is it advantageous for the company to outsource that business process? Has your company considered all alternatives to outsourcing? In some cases it may be determined in audit work that a function would be best served through outsourcing, i.e., "right-sourcing." However, we would find it very unusual for audit to suggest outsourcing since it is generally viewed as less control by the audit community. But in some cases it may be more controlled.

- The cost benefit analysis for outsourcing:

    - Does it make true economical sense to outsource the process taking into account the increased cost of monitoring, management, assurance, and reporting? Can management and audit rely on some of the control infrastructure supplied by the vendor?

- The contract development process:

    - Does the right to audit exist? Are there clear contract clauses that require specific performance and monitoring?

- Monitoring phase:

    - Is there a systematic audit program in place by the supplier to insure control objectives and contract compliance?

All of these points are expanded and discussed later in the book.

On October 25, 2002, a "Roundtable Discussion" on this topic was held at The University of Texas at Dallas. The participants were audit and accounting professionals who represented approximately 10 different companies. They were solicited for their opinions on "Best Practices" for auditing vendor relationships and specific controls that they would like to see implemented into an audit program for vendors. One of the main points to come out of the discussion was that auditors would like to have more involvement in all stages of the outsourcing process and that they need a more standardized program for completing the audit of outsourced situations. The aim of this Handbook is to provide a platform for auditor involvement and a general guideline for auditing vendor relations.

CHAPTER 1
BACKGROUND

Outsourcing, or strategic partnering as we know it, is not a new concept. Using the talent or resources of someone outside your organization is a concept that is basically as old as man himself. Civilizations have used conquered people to construct their cities, defend their walls, and produce their food since ancient times. These types of outsourcing arrangements were not done in a market system by private organizations; however, these empires basically outsourced for the same reasons companies continue to create partnerships today. Why would these people or any organization consider outsourcing?

- Lack of capital or resources
- Lack of labor
- Lack of technical knowledge about the process
- Increasing pressure to reduce costs
- Opportunity to increase focus on core competencies or value-added activities

These reasons for outsourcing are the same today as they were for our ancestors. Outsourcing is basically a response to a perceived need occurring within the organization. Ancient civilizations perceived that they needed to expand their empires in order to increase production capabilities, gain manpower, capture assets, and maintain their positions relative to their enemies. The theory was that these people could outsource areas in which they were not adept and therefore focus their efforts toward their strategic goals. This perceived need to outsource is examined later in the book when we talk about risks and risk analysis.

One could also argue that these empires faced the same challenges of outsourcing that many companies face today. Did the decision to outsource mesh with the entities' overall strategic plan? Did it make sense to outsource? How did they pick the outsource partner? Did they pick the right partner? Was there a thorough analysis of whether to keep the process in-house or outsource? Was there a rigorous and impartial selection process for the provider? Was a robust agreement drawn up and signed by all parties? Once the process was turned over, what assurance did the owner have that the job was being done and what systematic process did they implement to assure the task? Of course these ancient people did not operate under our current legal system and did not have the sophisticated decision-making strategies that we have today, but the basic ideas and obstacles still remain the same. These issues will be discussed later along with risk identification and mitigation.

As we move forward in our history, the idea of the centralized organization came into being and outsourcing decreased. The industrialization of mankind created the self-contained, self-sufficient organization. Early industrialists organized their factories to complete in-house any function that they needed. All processes were done in-house, from production to maintenance to storage of the finished product. It was not until recently that outsourcing as we know it once again gained popularity. Companies slowly began to realize that they should focus only on core activities and divest themselves of non-core functions. For the reasons that we mentioned earlier, companies began to realize that in order to stay competitive, they needed to focus on those areas that gave them the most advantage in the marketplace. During the early reintroduction of outsourcing, companies mainly joined forces with partners who could bring expertise to the organization that was not available in-house. These types of partnerships allowed access to production capabilities, delivery and storage services, and computer assistance. Once other companies began to learn about these partnerships, they also decided to join the march toward the virtual company.

The idea of divesting yourself of non-core functions seems to make sense on the surface. Some argue that all non-core functions should be outsourced. However, new risks are created when the decision to outsource is implemented. One of the risks your organization faces is that the outsourcing does not strategically align with your objectives. You must really understand your core competencies and what constitutes a core function. In order to completely understand what functions are not critical to your mission or what functions do not add to your competitive advantage, your organization must have a robust and complete strategic plan. The idea to outsource and the identification of what process to outsource are examined in later chapters.

This leads us to current times. As this is written, the trend toward outsourcing continues. As we previously stated, many believe that the future organization should resemble something called a "virtual company." This "virtual company" would be shed of all functions that were not core to its strategic mission, leaving the company to focus all of its energies toward its main core competencies. The "virtual company" would have identified the function that enables it to maintain a competitive advantage in the marketplace and would focus on leveraging that competency. We believe one of the flaws with this virtual company is the fallacy that it could mainly focus on its core competency and forget about non-core functions. Just because something is outsourced, it does not alleviate management from the responsibility for the process. It does create an environment that can potentially be prone to a breakdown in controls with a lack of communication. This breakdown can result from the vendor being pressed to reduce costs. An argument could be made that if you divest yourself of all functions, you have changed your control environment outside the organization, thereby creating more oversight and risk management. The more you outsource, the more you need governance, internal controls, and oversight. One of the biggest fallacies of outsourcing is that once you have turned over the process, you can move on to other tasks. Again more oversight may be costly up front, but a hands-off approach has spelled disaster for more than one company. An overall agreement with management, vendor, and auditor as to how the governance process will work in the new environment creates the right steps for the change in the control environment.

As we see, many risks begin to emerge when discussing outsourcing. The auditor should be aware of these risks and should be involved with outsourcing from the initiation stage to the assurance stage. We are aware that most organizations do not involve internal audit in the early stages of outsourcing. In a recent survey, the respondents were asked: "Does the internal audit department get involved with the decision-making process for the creation of an outsourcing partnership?" Over 72% answered "No." We believe that internal auditors should be involved since they are the gatekeepers who will assure that internal controls are meeting managements' goals and objectives. Overall, outsourcing creates a tremendous opportunity for internal audit to add value to the process by assisting management with due diligence, thereby creating a successful partnership. With this brief background in mind, let us begin to look at the process for understanding and assuring a vendor relationship.

CHAPTER 2
A SUCCESSFUL MARRIAGE

Before we begin to talk about tools for identifying risks, mitigation techniques, and audit procedures, we should spend a few minutes on relationship building. Building a good relationship with the vendor is probably the most important factor in ensuring a successful partnership. Many of the things that go wrong in an outsourcing relationship flow from some of the same problems that exist in any relationship — no self analysis for strengths and weaknesses, miscommunication, incompatible goals and expectations, unclear boundaries, confusion about responsibilities, unsure how to resolve conflict, win/lose attitudes, incompatible priorities, empathy, and so forth. This is another area where the auditor has a chance to assist management with evaluations and alignments before a process is outsourced. Management needs to address the relationship concerns and document their understanding in order for the partnership to be successful. So many times organizations rush into outsourcing because the short-run momentum to cut costs overshadows the necessity to search out compatible partners that have the same goals and objectives. As we all know, choosing a partner without thorough forethought and level thinking leads to disaster.

The auditor can add value to the outsourcing process by helping management identify those factors that make a successful marriage. The auditor can further benefit management by assessing those factors that maintain a successful relationship after it has been established. Management must not enter into a good relationship and then let it sour because they have neglected to follow some common guidelines for a happy partnership. The organization should consider carefully how they manage the relationship once it is established. One of the first mistakes that many organizations make is choosing the wrong relationship manager for the outsourced process. Most organizations will leave the person that was once in charge of the process in the role of overseeing the vendor. While the former manager may have the technical knowledge to effectively run the process, he or she may not have the necessary tools needed to oversee and work effectively with the vendor. Having people skills and negotiating skills is different from being able to manage a process. The organization should put careful consideration into the team that they employ to oversee the vendor.

Creating a solid partnership is almost an art form. Many of the success factors are reliant on intangible skills that different people bring to the table. The internal auditor can add value to the process by making management aware of the factors and helping to ensure that the correct people with the proper skill sets are involved with the process. Those people should understand that creating an outsourcing agreement is a major change for the organization — and change is difficult even under the best of circumstances. The auditor needs to ensure that management is aware that change brings with it special risks and that those risks are addressed. Many people within the organization, especially those that had prior involvement with the process, are going to resist the change. This resistance could lead to difficulties with the relationship. The auditor needs to be observant for attitudes surrounding the outsourced process. Management must be made aware of possible turf battles between the internal team and the vendor. Human nature tends toward the "silo effect." This phenomenon occurs in a changing environment, where individuals become protective of the process and uncooperative with those involved with the migration. In some instances, individuals can go beyond noncooperation to sabotage. The auditor needs to be on the lookout for general attitudes surrounding the vendor and their oversight. An opportunity exists in the early stages of discussion with vendors for the internal auditors or others familiar with the control environment to discuss how key control features will work as part of the outsource arrangement.

In summary, a good outsourcing relationship should be created with a win/win mentality. The auditor can assure this by helping management understand their strategic goals and assessing whether the outsourcing process aligns with those goals and strategies. Too many times, organizations engage vendors solely on a low price basis. As we all know, price cannot be the only factor involved when discussing what is best for the organization. Many times it may make sense to ignore price in the short run to gain access to a technique or process that the organization cannot provide in-house. If the goal is to capture the advantage of a new technique, price may not be the driver. Also, selecting a vendor based solely on cost may lead to some negative consequences such as an ineffective control environment, lack of information security, and poor quality assurance. Each of these has a cost associated with them and someone needs to pay. In any case, a partnership cannot be based solely upon one driver. With the help of internal audit, management can examine all their strengths and weaknesses and make an informed decision when it comes to creating a successful marriage.

Best Practices for a Solid Relationship

- Self-analysis (strengths and weaknesses brought to the partnership).
- Establish good communication.
- Ensure compatible goals and expectations (alignment with strategic plan).
- Set clear boundaries.
- Clearly delineate responsibilities.
- Plan for conflict resolution.
- Have a win/win attitude.
- Select the proper relationship manager/s.

- Be vigilant for poor attitudes.
- Have a clear monitoring plan.
- Establish regular dialogue about the relationship and the status.
- Have a clear exit strategy.

If internal auditors from either the outsource provider or client find some of these areas clearly lacking, an opportunity exists for them to quickly consult with management to address the specific issue.

Management faces many risks if the relationship with the vendor is not initiated properly and monitored with care. The organization should truly look at the vendor as a marriage partner. This is an company that potentially has access to intimate details about the organization. They are going to process work for the organization that is hopefully completed in a timely, effective, and accurate manner. The organization is relying on them to be honest, trustworthy, and loyal. Surely it is in the best interest of the organization to ensure that the vendor also perceives the relationship to be a win for them. Proper relationship building is truly the most important place for the internal audit staff to have a value-added impact. Once a contract is in place, the potential to mitigate risk in the inception has passed. Internal auditors' involvement from the beginning can help ensure success and value can be added.

CHAPTER 3
ISSUES AND CONTROL
OBJECTIVES

The purpose of this chapter is to familiarize the reader with some of the issues and control objectives that relate to outsourcing situations. The development of any audit plan should begin with an understanding of these issues and the control objectives that management has put in place. The reasons for outsourcing are various and implementation and monitoring are not always consistent. The auditor should consider the following issues when deciding on an audit plan:

- When and how was the decision to outsource made?
- At what level of the organization did the outsourcing decision emanate?
- Was a cost benefit analysis done and documented?
- Did the company consider keeping the process in-house?
- Were other alternatives considered, i.e., cosourcing, etc.?
- Was a unique contract completed with a detailed service-level agreement?
- Does the contract have the right to audit?
- Does a plan exist to bring the process back in-house if the vendor is no longer able to complete the engagement?
- Does the vendor have a contingency plan in case of catastrophic failure?

What generated the decision to outsource? The auditor should always be interested in knowing and understanding why outsourcing was considered. The following are some of the reasons that management will give for outsourcing, along with questions that should be addressed:

- Outsourcing can reduce our cycle times.
  - Possibly, but was an analysis documented and completed to show this comparison?

- Outsourcing can free us from a non-core, repetitive process.
  - Possibly, but does the decision to outsource truly align with the overall strategic plan and is the process truly non-core when compared to the plan?

- We can take advantage of our partner's economies of scale.
  - Ensure that there is an analysis to back this statement.

- We can transfer the process and minimize our investment.
  - This may be true if it is a new process, but what about the long-run financial impact?

- This will improve efficiency.
  - Verify the model that is being used for comparison. Could be response times, production cycles, etc.

- Use of outsourcing will give us access to advanced technology.
  - This could be true, but what is the goal that the process is achieving and could it be accomplished without the advanced technology?

- Outsourcing eliminates our expertise shortage.
  - Outsourcing can provide access to expertise that you do not have in-house; however, the auditor must verify that this expertise is needed and that the benefit outweighs the cost.

- Outsourcing helps facilitate downsizing.
  - Outsourcing can assist a company when it needs to contract; however, the risk it creates is that once the

process is outsourced and the company is smaller, who will have the in-house expertise to oversee the process?

These are just some of the advantages that management will attribute to outsourcing. Most of the advantages are true, but the auditor's job is to make sure that these alleged advantages are truly verifiable. The adage for auditors is always the same, "Trust, but verify."

Outsourcing also has many disadvantages and the auditor needs to keep them in mind when developing an audit plan. Some of the disadvantages are:

- Outsourcing expands the control environment beyond the original parameters.
- Sometimes key control issues are given up when a company outsources.
- Your trusted partner or vendor may breach your confidentiality.
- You may lose key personnel to the vendor.
- Vendor may show a lack of responsiveness.
- There is always the potential for additional service charges.
- Outsourcing creates the risk of difficulty of bringing it back in-house or moving to another vendor.

All of the above can be disadvantages to outsourcing, but the auditor should look at this list as an opportunity to add value to the process. Internal audit can help management to mitigate and eliminate many of these disadvantages through risk management and due diligence. Throughout this Handbook we discuss techniques to mitigate these disadvantages, such as audit involvement throughout the process, effective communication, proper contract administration, and so forth.

At what level did the decision to outsource emanate? The auditor needs to be aware of the level at which the outsourcing decision was generated. According to our survey, over 70% of the time the decision to outsource was generated by upper management. The auditor needs to be aware of how this decision-making process was started in order to understand the need analysis for outsourcing. The auditor should probe for related-party transactions and look for evidence of enticements in the form of gifts, trips, kickbacks, and so forth. In some instances, the outsourcing agreement is initiated and pursued by the vendor. Some departments within the organization, such as purchasing, may have strong relationships with vendors and these relationships could be leveraged into unsatisfactory outsourcing agreements without a rigorous selection process. The auditor should gain an understanding of how this outsourcing arrangement aligns with the company's overall strategy. Does this arrangement fit the goals and objectives of the organization? That is why the authors recommend an overall review of the company's outsourcing practices and get management buy-in to policies and practices. The framework of these actions and controls should be communicated throughout the enterprise so that all employees are clear on the "rules" of outsourcing.

What about cost benefit analysis? The auditor needs to determine if a cost benefit analysis was completed prior to the signing of the final contracts for the outsourcing agreement. In too many cases we have found that internal audit was not involved in the decision analysis or review. This statement is one of the common themes discovered through the survey process. In the comment section of the survey, we regularly received the following type of response: "Internal audit does and has audited outsourced arrangements post-implementation." As auditors, it is apparent that post-implementation is not the time to become involved. If due diligence is not performed throughout the entire process, efficiency, effectiveness, and economy cannot be achieved on a regular basis. For example, without a cost benefit analysis, there is no assurance or documentation to prove that it was more economical to outsource the process. Also, it was noted that very little benchmarking was done to continually measure the performance of the vendor along with cost trends. Although some management groups may require this, it is always a practice for some goods and services. As an example, the ongoing price increases when you have knowledge that products such as computers have a significant decrease in price through performance improvements.

Was there a discussion to keep the process in-house? Is there evidence of a thorough discussion regarding the possibility of keeping the process in-house or the viability and ongoing review of particular vendors before making the outsourcing agreement? The auditor needs to be aware that management has a responsibility to discuss keeping the process in-house before taking the risk of creating an outsourcing arrangement. Many times, the risk of losing knowledgeable employees and releasing key control of a process can outweigh the alleged cost savings of outsourcing. The auditor should look for evidence that suggests these issues were considered.

Is there a "unique contract" for the agreement? In many cases, companies have either used contracts from the vendor or no contract at all to set up outsourcing agreements. During the Dot-Com rise, companies were notorious for using personal networks to make contact with outsourcers and then setting up the agreement with a simple meeting and a handshake. When the bubble started to burst, many companies were left with no IT support, equipment, or personnel. Worst of all they did not have a written contract that may have helped with the situation.

The use of vendor favorable contracts is another issue that the auditor should be aware of and the preference of management is to use a contract that has been approved by your firms' legal representation. When time constraints are pushing the process, it is easy for some employees to submit blanket contracts instead of agreements that are customized to the situation. Each outsourcing agreement should ensure that it is customized to the unique characteristics of the arrangement. If blanket contracts are used, the organization runs the risk of creating expectation gaps for the client and the vendor. Creating a contract from scratch may not be feasible in every case. Cost and the size of the contract may not dictate a white paper contract. The auditor simply needs to be aware that each scenario is different and in some cases it may be acceptable to use standard contract language. As auditors, we would simply like to see documentation verifying the analysis process for selecting contract language that is not unique to the situation.

Does the contract have the right to audit? Surprisingly, the survey that was conducted revealed the fact that many companies forget or do not wish to include the right to audit for fear that it may hold up the negotiations. All outsourcing contracts must contain the right to audit, even if the company has no intention of auditing the process. Again, the objectives of economy, efficiency, and effectiveness cannot be achieved without a systematic and thorough audit. Without the right to audit, all power transfers to the vendor. They have control of the process and the right to keep you from it. This could potentially result in management's intention not being achieved.

Has the company considered contract termination? Contract termination occurs when the vendor quits providing service or you decide it is best to end the contract. Building as many potential scenarios into the contract that allow your company alternatives to discontinue the contract is imperative. Has your company planned for this contingency? Planning in advance for alternatives is key in providing smooth and uninterrupted transition to services. The auditor should look for evidence that the company is aware of terms providing for contract reversal and has a plan in place to deal with this situation. Typically, key knowledgeable personnel are no longer working in-house because the process was outsourced. Can the company restart the process or provide this service through another provider. What would be the downtime? These and other issues must be addressed.

Is there a vendor contingency plan? Not only does your company need to have a documented contingency plan, but the vendor also needs to provide evidence of a plan for continuous service in the event of an outage or catastrophe. This is a step that is typically considered post-implementation. However, it is a step that your company cannot afford to be without and may drive up the costs after contingency issues are considered. Due diligence would dictate that in a risk-based assessment, an auditor would want to see that the vendor will still be able to provide service in the unlikely event of a disaster. Contingency planning is key for your vendors. Their failure in a time of crisis could mean failure for you also. The auditor needs to assure that the contract has a clause requiring the vendor to have a contingency plan, and the contract needs to delineate what that plan must entail. At a minimum, the clause should state that the vendor will:

- Express the state of their contingency plan in writing.
- Provide their understanding in writing of what is "mission critical" for the process.
- Provide timely updates to evidence readiness.
- State their policy for backups of electronic media and the locations of the backups.
- State their plan for obtaining backup equipment if it is critical to the mission.
- Provide names and alternate numbers of key personnel responsible for continuing service in a crisis situation.
- State their plans for alternate means of communication in the event of failure.

These are just some of the issues that should be addressed in the vendor's contingency plan. This list is not intended to be all-inclusive but is intended to give the auditor some guidelines for what a thorough plan should contain.

The issues we have discussed are important because they give the auditor a basic understanding and framework to begin a plan for the audit. It is also important for the auditor to gain an understanding of the objectives of the outsourced process along with the objectives of the outsourcing arrangement. Once a process has been outsourced, the audit work has now been expanded to gaining an understanding of two separate and distinct objectives. If, for example, the purchasing function were to be outsourced, the auditor would need to have a documented understanding of the basic objectives of that department along with a separate understanding of the objectives of the outsourcing arrangement. We would argue once again that the process of outsourcing does not decrease the entire workload for the company but increases the work scope for the auditor. The auditor now has two sets of objectives that must be satisfied, documented, and understood. It is not enough to understand that the objective of the purchasing function is to procure raw materials for a competitive price at the moment they are needed. The auditor must ensure that management control processes are in place to ensure the vendor is meeting the objectives. Management will argue that the control objectives of the purchasing function remain the same post-outsourcing; however, the old objectives are now coupled with the new goals. The auditor must now also ensure that the proper vendor was selected at a competitive price and that they have the skill sets to complete the task within the contract provisions.

The comparison chart below illustrates this:

Objectives of the purchasing function department prior to outsourcing arrangement:

- Procure materials.
- Obtain competitive prices for materials purchased.
- Ensure that materials are available when needed.

Objectives post-outsourcing:

- Procure materials.
- Obtain competitive prices for material purchased.
- Ensure that materials are available when needed.
- Ensure competitive bidding process for selection of vendor.
- Ensure vendor has the capabilities to complete the services required.
- Ensure vendor is meeting service-level agreements.
- Ensure vendor has controls in place to assure process meets company's internal objectives.

These are examples of the objectives of a specific process prior to outsourcing and post-outsourcing. The objectives of the process remain the same, but after outsourcing, the previous objectives become a subset of the outsourcing objectives. If the vendor does not meet the above objectives, then the process is possibly not efficient or effective. The very process of outsourcing may reduce the number of employees and eliminate the process internally for the company, but it has the opposite effect of expanding the control environment for which management is responsible. This expansion of the control environment creates additional risk that must be addressed, and steps can be taken to minimize the possible impacts. In the next chapter we examine the risks that are common in outsourcing relationships and begin to build our risk-based audit model.

CHAPTER 4
RISK ANALYSIS

As we have already mentioned, outsourcing has some unique and varying risks depending upon the type of process that is outsourced. The risks that are inherent with outsourcing can be unique to each situation; however, there are some common risks that we can address and plan for in establishing controls. The main focus of this chapter is to assist the auditor with the risk identification process. The auditor must remember to analyze each situation and develop a risk analysis based upon the process that is being audited.

The risks that are encountered when outsourcing can vary depending upon the industry and the process that is being turned over to a trusted vendor. The chart below briefly illustrates some of those industries, processes, and risks. This chart gives the reader a visual representation of the processes that can be outsourced. It helps in illustrating that while some processes may be routine and non-core-related for some industries, other industries may see process as giving them a competitive advantage in the marketplace. As an example, the financial industry may identify supply chain management as routine and low risk level for their particular needs. However, a manufacturing firm may identify supply chain management as the critical function that allows them to maintain a competitive advantage over their competitors in the marketplace. The auditor should use this chart to assist in the process of gaining an understanding of the types of industry involved in the audit, the types of possible processes that could be outsourced, and the risks associated with those processes.

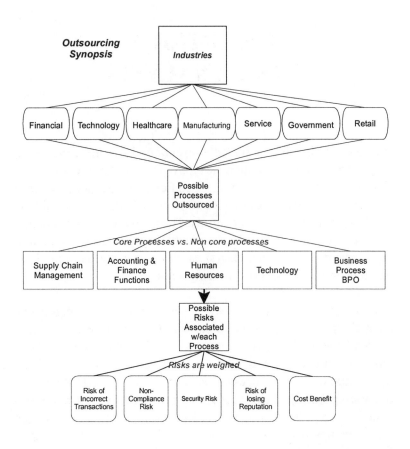

The risks that are shown in the chart are not all-inclusive and can change with each scenario. The important point is to make sure that the auditor assists management in identifying and documenting the risks that are associated with the outsourcing decision.

Even though the risks can be unique for every situation, we now present the auditor with a list of common issues and risks that are basically encountered with every outsourcing arrangement. This list can assist with the development of proper controls that will enable management to achieve their objectives. The list is also valuable for gaining an understanding of the area under review. Some of the issues and risks inherent with outsourcing are:

- Business risks
- Contract risks
- Transaction risks
- Risk to reputation
- Noncompliance and legal risk
- Strategic risk
- Security risk
- Vendor risk

The Business Factors

The business risk relates to the potential that the outsourcing decision does not align with your overall strategic goals. If outsourcing a process is not compatible with your strategic goals or initiatives, your organization may lose earnings or assets. If your organization does not have a thorough understanding of each of these factors, the decision to outsource should be put on hold. Gaining an understanding of each of these issues is critical before deciding to outsource. Some of the business issues to consider are:

Financial Standards for Vendor	Disputes/Terminations	Billing Provisions
Quality Assurance Term of Contract	Confidentiality Security	Personnel Additional Services
Regulatory Compliance	Division of Responsibilities	Asset Ownership

Financial Standards for the Vendor — Engaging a vendor that is not a viable ongoing concern is a tremendous business risk for an organization. It seems simple to point out that there is a risk that the vendor may not be financially stable, but it is a risk that must be addressed when selecting a partner.

Disputes and Termination — There is a risk that the issue of disputes and termination has not been properly addressed in the contracting phase. How will the organization handle disputes and how can this relationship be terminated?

Billing Provisions — An auditor needs to be aware that detailed and documented billing provisions must be in the contract. A lack of a detailed billing provision can lead to overpayment.

Quality Assurance — QA is an extremely important issue when deciding upon outsourcing. How will the organization assure that quality is maintained? If the process is relatively simple, the risk is not as great. If the process is a highly complex and technical task, then the organization faces a large risk in turning over this line of work. A highly complex task may be a core competency of the firm and the auditor needs to examine whether or not this process should have been turned over in the first place. NASA is famous for outsourcing highly technical tasks and, as the Challenger explosion illustrated, the lack of oversight of the vendor can have serious consequences. The manufacturing of complex parts requires extreme internal controls at the client level and at the vendor level. Once NASA relinquished control of the process, they relinquished quality control in this instance. This is an extreme example, and it is used to merely illustrate the risks inherent with quality assurance. An organization must be aware that once it has engaged in outsourcing, it has not relinquished ownership. Taking full responsibility for the finished product or process is still the responsibility of the organization. As we will discuss later, one of the inherent risks associated with outsourcing is the tendency for individuals and the organization to turn their back on the process and let the vendor assume full responsibility for the completion and oversight of the process. This type of attitude can have serious consequences and the organization must be on guard to prevent it.

Confidentiality — Once an outsource arrangement has been finalized, the client faces the risk that the vendor may breach their trust. The vendor can coop proprietary methods or information. The vendor may also violate the client's trust by releasing confidential data about the client. The auditor needs to be aware of this risk and look for the proper controls in the contract.

Personnel — Personnel changes are always an issue when outsourcing. The issue becomes who will the client keep to oversee the process and who are the personnel that are working for the vendor? There is a risk that the client will keep too many, not enough, and the wrong people to oversee the process. Alternatively, there is an issue that the vendor may not have enough knowledgeable staff to effectively complete the task. The client also faces the risk that the vendor may "steal" away the clients' key personnel. The auditor needs to be aware of these issues and look for controls that are in place to address the consequences. Loss of personnel can occur at anytime and the auditor can assist management by ensuring that they have considered and put into place a good communication plan that makes personnel feel involved with the process and keeps them up to date on the status of the organization. Audit should ensure that management is continuously involved with personnel and the morale within the organization.

Term — There is a risk that a client may enter into a contract with a vendor for a term that does not fit the strategic plan for the client. The term can be too long or, in some cases, it may not be long enough. Deciding upon the correct term length of the contract requires due diligence for the long-range strategic plan of the organization. The length of the contract must be auditable against some rationale for the decision. Typically, this rationale would have something to do with a documented long-range plan. Being locked into a long-term contract with an undesirable partner who is not performing up to the service-level agreement can have devastating effects on the organization. The auditor should probe for the rationale behind the term decision.

Security — Security is a major issue in this post 9-11 world. It is imperative that the vendor has documented security standards that are available for the client auditor to review. Security can include access to assets, data, or proprietary methods. The client should identify those areas that represent security risks for the process and require that the vendor acknowledge those risks and have a plan in place to minimize them.

Additional Services — Invariably, whenever your organization enters into an outsourcing arrangement, the issue of additional services is going to arise. If the contract process is not well thought out, the organization runs the risk of having the vendor charge them for "additional services" not included in the contract. This can become extremely frustrating and costly for the client. The auditor needs to gain an independent understanding of the process and audit it to the contract to ensure that there are not gaping holes in the service-level agreement. It is very easy to forget a service clause in the contract if the process is complex and technical in nature.

Regulatory Compliance — In some instances, your organization can face the risk of regulatory noncompliance from a vendor. If the process you have outsourced has regulatory restraints, your organization is obligated to ensure that the vendor is following those regulations. The auditor needs to examine the contract to ensure that it mentions the regulatory compliance. An auditor also needs to see documented evidence from the vendor that they are aware of the regulation and are in compliance. The vendor's failure to comply with regulations can have serious consequences for the organization and, in some cases, for upper management.

Division of Responsibility — One of the major risks encountered in outsourcing is the lack of a clear delineation of which party is responsible for what portion of the process. If the contract is not detailed and clear, the vendor may become confused about which part of the process they are responsible for and the requirements for completion. An auditor should examine management's understanding of which part of the process has been turned over and then should look to the vendor to see if they have acknowledged responsibility for the entire process. Problems can arise in this area because the client may keep too much of the process in-house and not turn over the work to the vendor, creating a situation where neither party is effectively completing the process. In order to be successful in this area, internal audit can help management assess how much of the process must be turned over in order for the relationship to meet the criteria of being effective, efficient, and accurate. Internal audit should conduct and audit the process and examine it for any unforeseen connections within the organization. How much of the process is truly autonomous and how much of it could affect other departments if it is suddenly missing from the picture? The migration of a process to a vendor does not happen in a vacuum and management must be made aware of the details of the process and the possible in-house connections and their impact.

Asset Ownership — Another risk that you encounter when outsourcing is that the ownership of certain assets can become confused. For example, if you transfer equipment and software to the vendor, you must have a clear, documented chain of ownership. Once equipment has been at the vendor's location for a period of time, the tendency is to forget about it. A gap analysis should be completed by internal audit after the transition period to true up ownership of assets related to the outsourced process. Internal audit can add value by helping management and the vendor both feel like they have been treated fairly in the transaction by verifying asset transfers under the contract. There needs to be a documented and systematic review of all assets that have been placed under the vendor's care, custody, and control. As a control check, the vendor should provide a timely report that lists any assets they hold for the client.

These are just some of the business factors to keep in mind when contemplating due diligence and assurance for outsourcing. Next we look at some more risks that arise when outsourcing.

The Contract

The contract is the most important piece of the outsourcing life cycle. Without a thorough, well thought out contract, the outsourcing arrangement is doomed to failure. The contracting process must take into account each situation as a discrete and independent process. The use of blanket contracts is not recommended for outsourcing agreements. In order to complete true due diligence, each outsourcing agreement must be analyzed and negotiated on its own merits. Too many organizations in the past have relied on blanket contracts and this has led to many unhappy partnerships. The contract is a breeding ground for risk if it is not contemplated in a systematic, rational manner. The following are some of the factors that an auditor should be aware of when recommending contract provisions or providing audit services:

- Blanket contract vs. unique
- Responsibilities clause
- Performance clause
- Service-level agreements
- Monitoring
- Inventory assets

- Delineation of assets and employees
- Confidentiality
- Term
- Right to audit

Many of these issues were mentioned along with business factors, but they bear repeating when discussing the contract. The development of the contract should proceed in a thoughtful and systematic manner. Adequate time should be given for both parties to negotiate the contract. If the contract is rushed because of time constraints, both parties need to take a step back and reexamine the process for possible alternatives. A hurried contract process can lead to potential trouble as time passes. We would argue that the internal auditors need to be involved with the contract phase in all cases. The internal auditors are going to provide the control assurance for management at a later date, so they also need to be involved with the due diligence phase of outsourcing.

As previously mentioned, each contract needs to be unique and not of a blanket nature. Use of blanket contracts can lead to gaping holes in the service level. The contract needs to clearly spell out the detailed responsibilities of both parties. If the responsibility clause is not clear, the vendor may not perform up to expected levels. The contract also needs to be clear on what responsibilities the client will have. Both parties need to document this understanding and keep the document on file. All contracts must contain the right to audit along with a monitoring clause. We understand that it is not feasible for all organizations to audit all of their vendor relations. One survey respondent indicated that their company had over 88,000 vendors. The auditor must make sure that the contract has the right to audit because a particular vendor may become a high risk and may be put on the list for closer monitoring. More about vendor ranking and risk management will be discussed in a later chapter.

All outsourcing contracts should include an inventory of assets and the specified location of such assets. Both parties should sign off on the list and the vendor should be required to provide timely reports outlining those assets that have been placed in their care. The contract should also be clear on staffing issues. An understanding should be documented about which employees are responsible for the process at the client and at the vendor's location. If these issues are not addressed, the company exposes itself to loss of assets or wasted resources.

Another important issue that has been mentioned is the term of the contract. The term of the contract can create the risk of being locked into an unfavorable position for an undesirable amount of time, and it should be given careful consideration. The auditor should look for evidence of an analysis to show how the term of the contract aligns with the strategic plan of the organization. The term of the contract must have a relationship to a documented analysis.

Transaction Risk — If due diligence and proper controls are not implemented, your organization faces the risk of loss due to incorrect transactions by the vendor. Releasing an internal process to a third party creates the risk that the vendor may or may not complete your transactions properly. Depending upon the process that is being completed by the vendor, incorrect transactions can have serious consequences to your organization. Later we will discuss mitigation techniques to manage the risk of incorrect transactions.

Reputation Risk — One of the biggest risks an organization faces when it relinquishes control of a process is the risk to its reputation. The organization is now relying on a third party to maintain its reputation by continuing to provide service or products that are of the customary standards. An auditor needs to be aware of this risk and look for controls that have been put in place to minimize the effects.

Noncompliance and Legal Risk — Anytime an outsourcing agreement is made, the client exposes himself or herself to the risk that the vendor may be engaged in illegal activities, or the vendor may not comply with regulations resulting in legal action. The client is now linked to a third party in whom they have no oversight for the internal control environment. This lack of control is why it is extremely important to have the right to audit and the right to see documented evidence of the vendor's internal control systems. Your organization needs to spend time during the selection process talking with the potential vendors and asking questions about their attitude toward internal control. If a potential vendor seems resistant to requests for internal control documentation, then they should be immediately eliminated from the list. Exposure to lawsuit is a risk that everyone is aware of, but steps need to be taken to manage the risk. We will address risk management steps in the next few chapters.

Vendor Risk — Finally, one of the last risks we will address is one that is associated with the vendor. The risks that we have discussed so far have been associated with the selection process, due diligence, and monitoring. There is also an inherent risk that a current vendor may become unstable and fail. Once a vendor has been put in place, continuous monitoring needs to occur to ensure that the vendor remains a viable ongoing concern. If your organization does not systematically monitor vendors for stability, you will have no early warning in the event of a failure. Vendors must be assessed and ranked according to their risk to your organization and the overall risk of the vendors' operations.

In summary, outsourcing can be a risky endeavor. Each process has its own level of risk and mitigation factors. The auditor simply needs to be aware that whenever outsourcing is mentioned, there must be documented discussion of the risk factors. At a minimum, the organization should recognize and document the risk exposure from:

- Incorrect transactions.
- Noncompliance.
- Business risk (risk that outsourcing does not align with your strategic goals and objectives).
- Potential risk to reputation.

Outsourcing can expose the organization to many other risks, but a majority of them fall within the preceding four categories. However, each process needs to be examined independently for risk analysis. Some of the other risks your organization may encounter are risk to credit and political risk when your organization conducts business internationally. These are just some of the risks you may find. As we have mentioned, any due diligence process should include a risk assessment for the process that is being considered. Risks usually arise because of poor planning and lack of due diligence. Our aim is to ensure that your organization approaches the outsourcing decision with a systematic and rational plan.

Identification of risk is one of the steps to be completed during due diligence. The next step involves the process of establishing risk mitigation techniques and a control structure to minimize the impact of the identified risk. We discuss risk and control in the next chapter.

CHAPTER 5
RISK STRATEGIES

Now that we have identified some of the potential risks of outsourcing, let's take a look at strategies for minimizing the impact of those risk exposures. Below you will find a table that outlines some possible steps that the auditor could take to identify and rank risk and exposure. This table assists you in focusing your time and efforts on those risks that have the greatest potential for a negative impact.

Process Outsourced	Potential Risks	Complexity	Internal Controls	Internal Audit Priority
Business Process (Mail Room Functions)	Transactional Reputational	Low	Low-Medium Low-Medium	Low Low
Human Resources	Noncompliance	Medium	Medium	Moderate
Technology	Security Transactional Noncompliance Reputation	High	High	High
Accounting or Finance	Transactional Noncompliance Security Reputational	Medium-High	High	Moderate-High

The items that are listed in the table are not all-inclusive or exhaustive, they are merely presented in an effort to provide a framework that could be used when assessing risk for vendor relations. The table presents examples of areas that could be outsourced, then moves on to typical risks that are encountered with the process. Next we rank the complexity of the area that is outsourced. How involved is the process that has been outsourced? Is the process a routine and repetitive task or is it one that is highly complex and requires proprietary knowledge? As we have discussed, risk and the need for control increases with the complexity of the task. Once you have identified the potential risks and the level of complexity, the auditor can assess the need for internal control. The auditor can also use the chart as a benchmark for determining the time commitment needed to assure the process. As the table illustrates, simple processes are low risk and do not require high priority from internal audit.

Now that we have identified the level of risks that are involved with outsourcing, how can the internal auditor assist management in controlling and mitigating the potential impact of those risks? When deciding upon a strategy for dealing with risk, you have a number of choices:

- Accept the risk.
- Avoid the risk.
- Manage or transfer the risk.

For the purposes of this Handbook, we will focus our attention on avoiding or managing the risk of outsourcing. As previously mentioned, risk is usually created through poor planning and lack of due diligence. We believe that with proper due diligence most of the risk of outsourcing can be avoided. Some might ask, "What do we do with legacy outsourcing agreements?" (Outsourcing arrangements that were made in the past and are still in place.) In those instances, we will use the technique of risk management or minimization.

Let's begin by focusing on the process of risk avoidance. We have already identified some categories of risk for outsourcing that include:

- Transactional risk.
- Noncompliance risk.
- Risk to the organizations' reputation, etc.
- Lack of internal control (clients or vendors).

The question becomes how do we avoid these risks. The process includes planning and due diligence. We need to begin by asking a series of questions:

- Why do we need to outsource?
- What prompted the decision to outsource?
- Do we have a document in place that can guide the process?
- Do we have content experts on staff to assist and oversee the process?
- Do we have methods for selecting vendors?
- Do we understand the risks inherent in outsourcing?
- Once we have outsourced, do we have competent staff to oversee the arrangement?
- Are there legal or regulatory requirements for outsourcing this process? (banking, energy, government, etc.)
- Is there a contingency plan in the event that the vendor fails?

These are just some of the questions to ask and they provide us with a place to start our process. Above all we urge the internal audit department to be involved with the outsourcing process from inception all the way through monitoring. Our survey indicates that most internal auditors would agree and would like to be involved from the moment that outsourcing is considered. The questionnaire confirmed the fact that most internal audit departments are brought in after the fact and are simply in a monitoring position, or they are brought in when the arrangement has gone bad.

Risk avoidance begins with due diligence and we have included a flowchart below that illustrates the possible steps to include when initiating the outsourcing process.

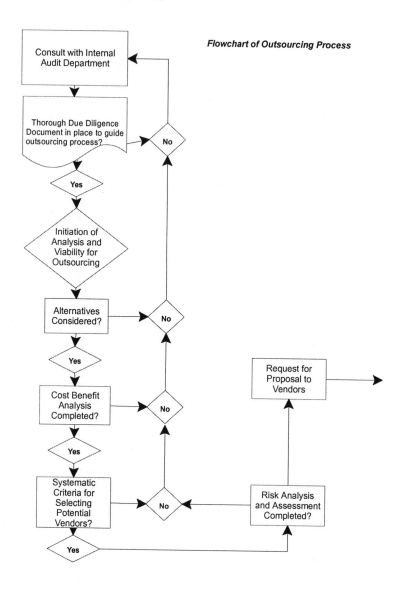

Flowchart of Outsourcing Process

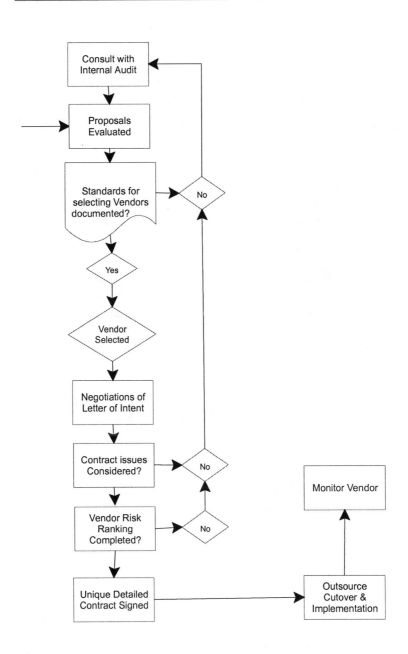

The flowcharting process should also include plans for recapturing the process in the event of dissolution with the vendor. The risk of having to bring the process back in-house is extremely high when outsourcing. Once the process has been relinquished, it is very difficult to recover it effectively and efficiently without a well thought out prior plan.

We believe that any thorough due diligence process should begin by consulting with internal audit about the outsourcing arrangement. Internal audit can begin by assessing the organization's needs and gaining an understanding of the process. Let's address some of the specific risks and avoidance techniques.

Strategic Risk — The first risk we encounter is the risk that the outsourcing decision does not align with our strategic goals or plans. If we outsource processes that are critical to our business, a.k.a. core competencies, we stand to lose market share, revenue, trade secrets, and so forth. What can we do to avoid this risk? The auditor should check for:

- A documented strategic plan for the organization.
- An understanding of why outsourcing was considered.
- An analysis of where the outsource process fits into the long-range plan.
- An analysis of how outsourcing fits the strategic plan of the organization.
  - Are they attempting to become a virtual company?
  - Are they outsourcing only nonessential processes?
  - Are they attempting to create a strategy of strategic partnering by outsourcing?

Management must ensure that the decision to outsource aligns with the strategic plan of the organization. If management decides to outsource core competencies, a more thorough analysis should be documented and reviewed. The closer a process is to becoming a core competency, the higher the risk becomes for the organization if they relinquish control of that process. Core competencies are revealed through strategic planning and an organization should never seriously consider relinquishing control of a process that gives the organization a competitive advantage in the marketplace. We have noted through our research that more organizations are outsourcing critical functions now instead of outsourcing only non-core processes. This trend should result in more oversight and involvement from internal audit. If organizations are going to farm out their strengths, efficient, effective internal control will become more critical for the success of the arrangement.

Vendor Risk — After verifying that there are rational reasons for deciding to outsource, the organization should address the concern associated with vendor risk. Once you know you are going to outsource, there must be a systematic and rational system in place to determine vendor selection. The improper selection of a vendor exposes the organization to the risk of having service interrupted. To avoid this risk the organization should consider the following items when selecting a vendor:

- Relationship factors mentioned in Chapter 2
- Vendor reputation
- Experience level of vendor
- Qualifications
- Background of personnel at vendor
- Financials
- Internal control report
- Contingency planning of vendor
- Background of management team at vendor

As part of due diligence, there should be a documented procedure for an impartial vendor selection program. An auditor should investigate to see if there are any inducements from the vendor to key employees for the award of the contract. Management should also have documented the internal control environment of the vendor. Many organizations rely on SAS 70 reports for this documentation. SAS 70 reports are statements on auditing standards that were developed by the AICPA in response to a need for service organizations to provide positive assurance to their clients about the existence of internal controls. There are two types of SAS 70 reports: Type I and Type II. The main difference between the reports is that a Type II provides an opinion from the independent auditor about the operational effectiveness of the vendor's internal control environment to the point of providing reasonable assurance. Type II provides reasonable assurance that the controls are operating efficiently to achieve control objectives. This assurance is provided through testing. A Type I report, which is not as robust as Type II, merely points out that controls have been put in place as management has stated and that they are meeting specific control objectives. It should be pointed out that not all vendors provide SAS 70 reports, so management must make sure they request that the vendor show evidence of their internal controls. One of the quotes from a recent survey indicated that the client did not audit vendor relations because, "They rely heavily on the SAS 70 report." As we have seen, receiving a SAS 70 report and verifying the vendor's internal controls are only a small portion of due diligence when it comes to assuring vendor relations. Managements' attitude toward outsourcing must change and internal audit must be included in the outsourcing process from inception to monitoring.

Contract Risks — As we mentioned previously, if due diligence is not performed, the contract that is negotiated can result in a failed outsourcing arrangement. This type of failure can have serious consequences depending upon the type of process outsourced. Management must ensure that the contract development and negotiation process proceeds in a systematic and rational manner. The contract is the cornerstone of the outsourcing arrangement and must be thorough in order to have a successful partnership. A good contract process should include:

- Use of a unique contract — not a blanket form.
  - Never use blanket contracts. They cannot address unique situations.

- Agreed-upon terminology.
  - Make sure everyone agrees on terminology or language issues relating to the process.

- A term limit that is fair to both parties.
  - The length of the contract should have some bearing on the long-range goals of the client company.

- A clear delineation of duties and responsibilities.
  - Everyone must understand what portion of the process he or she will provide. The vendor must also confirm their understanding of the responsibilities of personnel working on the process, including employees that work for both the client and the provider.

- The right to audit
  - Key to contract. Every outsourcing agreement must contain the right to audit. We recognize that not all arrangements will receive the same level of due diligence; however, the client must always retain the right to audit. The marketplace today is an ever-changing, fast-paced environment and good risk management would dictate retaining all of your rights. We have included some generic language that the auditor might always look for in a standard "right to audit" clause. At a minimum, the clause should contain:

    - Name of the client and vendor.
    - Mention of reasonable access to vendor facilities.
    - For the purpose of conducting audits.

- Relevant to the vendor's performance and service and other matters related to the contract.
- In order to assure: Correct billing by vendor, verification of service levels for vendor, verification of all contract agreements for service.
- Timing of audits: once year, quarterly, etc.
- Proviso for more frequent audits if reasonably necessary.
- Audits may be during normal business hours.
- Vendor will cooperate with audit, providing documents requested in a timely manner, and will assist the auditors when necessary.
- Clause addressing additional services for audits if necessary.
- Clause requiring vendor to maintain records of process necessary for audit purposes.
- Confidentiality requirements for both parties.
- Clause detailing how the results of the audit will be addressed and reported.
- Clauses outlining how deficiencies discovered during audit will be resolved — who is responsible and to what extent.
- Clause outlining who will bear the cost of the audit.

The proceeding items are recommendations for issues that need to be addressed in a standard "right to audit" clause. The list is not meant to be all-inclusive or exhaustive. The list is provided to assist the auditor in verifying best practices under an outsourcing contract.

- Performance levels
    - Specifying performance levels provides the client with a monitoring tool. You now have a benchmark to judge vendor performance against.

- Clear compensation and fee structure
  - In order to avoid being charged for every additional service that arises after the contract is signed, management must make sure that compensation is clear and must have an agreement on the level and types of services that will be provided.

- Ownership clauses
  - The contract should specify what rights the vendor has to clients' assets, personnel, proprietary information, etc.

- Dispute resolution clause
  - In cases of disagreement, how will they be resolved? Consider using mediation, arbitration, etc.

- Confidentiality agreements
  - Ensure that the vendor is going to hold trade secrets and that they have internal controls in place that recognize this risk and have planned accordingly.

- Business continuity plans
  - Does the vendor have a contingency plan in case of interruption? Make sure there is a detailed written plan addressing this issue. In Chapter 2, we list items that should be found in all contingency plans.

- Insurance discussion
  - Consider request for vendor to provide evidence of commercial insurance covering negligence and business interruption.

- Termination clause
  - How can this contract be ended? Management should include details on contract termination.

- Assignment clause
  - Ensure that the vendor does not have the right to assign their duties under the contract.

Revenue Risk — When entering into an outsourcing arrangement, your organization always runs the risk of losing revenue because of poor planning or insufficient due diligence. In order to avoid this risk, management must employ the techniques mentioned above for strategic risk, vendor risk, and contract risk. In addition to those considerations, management must also conduct a cost/benefit analysis of the outsourcing decision. Many times, the short run savings of an outsourcing agreement can be outweighed by the failure of that agreement. It must make financial sense to enter into the agreement or the contract should not be signed. Many believe that outsourcing leads to the elimination of the costs associated with the process for the organization. This is not true, particularly in the short run. Not all costs go away just because a process has been outsourced. The organization needs to take into account the cost associated with overseeing the process once it is outsourced. In extreme cases, the cost associated with outsourcing, if calculated correctly, could exceed the perceived savings. The long-range goals of the organization must be taken into account and weighed against any short-term savings. Management must take into consideration that it may be more costly to oversee and monitor this arrangement than it is to keep it in-house. As we have argued, when you outsource, you are expanding the sphere of internal control and creating more risk. Sometimes this risk is very minimal but in other cases the risk is extreme and the control system needed to oversee it will increase accordingly. Management must be honest in their assessment of the resources that will be necessary to maintain the outsourcing relationship.

Strategic risk, vendor risk, and contract risk are all high-level issues and should be mitigated and avoided through proper due diligence. The risks associated with transactions, reputation, and compliance are all service-level risks and should be mitigated through the contracting and monitoring process.

Transaction Risk — The risk that the vendor will not properly execute your transactions can be mitigated through attention to detail in the contract and a thorough monitoring process. To minimize transactional risk, management should:

- Include detail expectations in the contract.
- Interview vendor personnel to ensure competence and understanding of the process.
- Require a systematic reporting system by vendor that indicates exceptions in transaction processing.
- Independently poll customers for satisfaction levels or complaints.
- Require regular face-to-face meetings with vendor to discuss system.
- Monitor service level on a regular basis.

These are just some of the techniques that management can employ to assure that transactions are processed properly. If the vendor begins to make mistakes, you can lose customers, market share, and value in your organization. Management must be vigilant toward the provider if the process is of a complex nature and core to the organization's structure.

At this point, it is also worth mentioning that there is a fine line between over-monitoring and the hands-off approach. In some instances, clients have been known to continuously monitor the vendor and cause the relationship to fail. If you have performed due diligence, you should be able to turn the process over to the vendor with the assurance that you have made the right decision.

Reputation Risk — As we mentioned earlier, if you chose the wrong vendor or your current vendor engages in activities that are illegal or unethical, you run the risk of losing the organization's hard-earned reputation. Before deciding to outsource, you should consider whether or not the process exposes you to losing your reputation. Once again, if the process is non-core and low complexity, there is very little risk exposure. However, if you choose to outsource a process that gives your organization its competitive advantage, you may lose your reputation if the vendor fails you. Some steps that management can take to ensure that the risk to your reputation is minimized or avoided:

- Only outsource those areas that are nonessential, and only areas that give you no competitive advantage.
- Confirm and verify the vendor's reputation in the marketplace.
- Confirm and verify the vendor's credit ranking.
- Confirm and verify the vendor's financial condition.
- Confirm vendor's attitude toward internal control and their internal control structure.
- Search for any pending litigation or claims against the vendor.
- Confirm the age of the vendor company.
- Interview top management and confirm attitudes.

Most companies have worked extremely hard to obtain their reputation in the marketplace. One bad outsourcing partnership can ruin that reputation. Due diligence must be conducted up front with the help of internal audit to ensure against this risk. No matter what the cost savings, it is never advisable to enter into a partnership with anyone who has shown unprofessional behavior or committed questionable acts.

Noncompliance Risk — This is the risk you face when the vendor does not comply with professional standards or laws and regulations. This risk also can occur because the vendor does not comply with the internal control procedures or policies. Noncompliance can have serious results for the vendor and your organization. If the vendor violates law or regulation, your organization could face serious fines or possible criminal charges. Management must take steps to minimize this risk if they are going to consider outsourcing. The following are some steps that management might take to manage this risk:

- Verify the vendor's reputation.
- Search for past violations.
- Include hold harmless agreements in the contract along with indemnification clauses.
- Specify penalties in the contract.
- Consider keeping in-house processes that are subject to stringent laws or regulations.
- Confirm the internal control structure of vendor.
- Interview vendor management for attitudes toward compliance.

Finally, since we realize that due diligence and auditing resources are limited, we would recommend assessing and ranking each vendor according to risk. Ranking the vendors would give management the opportunity to concentrate resources on those areas that present the greatest exposure. Vendors that receive the highest rankings would receive the most attention from auditing and would require the highest oversight. Vendor ranking should be done on an annual basis, during the annual audit plan meeting, or whenever a new vendor is added for the organization. We recommend consideration of the following factors when ranking vendors:

- Reputation of the vendor
- Complexity of process
- Number of risk exposures to the organization
- Core vs. non-core competency
- Financial condition of the vendor
- Can the vendor be easily replaced if they fail?
- Cost to bring process back in-house if contract reverses

- Ease of monitoring
- Credit rating of the vendor
- Responsiveness of the vendor to client needs
- Has the vendor documented and established internal controls specific to your process?
- Vendor's production of documentation verify internal controls
- Ease of access to the vendor and their audit team
- Does the vendor have internal audit staff?

The organization should continually monitor and update the vendor-ranking list to ensure that adequate attention is given to the highest risks.

Transition Period Risk — Once the decision to outsource has been made, the organization begins a transition period where the process begins to migrate to the vendor. During this period, the organization faces many risks surrounding the process. Decisions have to be made about the timing, preparation, and cutover period for the transition. In most instances, it is not possible for the migration to happen instantaneously and there can be a brief period where the process stops or is shared by the vendor and client. The auditor can ensure that management has considered and documented a plan to effectively migrate the process to the vendor. As we have previously discussed, the more complex the process is, the more difficult the transition will be and the more risk will emerge if not handled properly. Internal audit should verify that management has assessed the process and established a baseline activity mode for the work. What is the minimum amount of the process that must be accomplished within a specified time period without incurring a material negative impact? This is the question that internal audit can help management establish. Internal audit needs to make management aware that the transition period is a time when employee morale may be most affected. Management needs to have an effective communication plan in place to ensure that employees are informed and that they feel like they are part of the process for the transition. The communication plan needs to detail for the employees what is the future status of the outsourced process. The auditor can verify that management has trained the proper personnel to oversee the process once it has been outsourced and ensure that those personnel are already available.

Managing the risk imposed by your providers is a task that is required for the continued success of the organization. Once an organization has decided to enter into the outsourcing arena, it must be ready to deal with the exposures that come from relinquishing control of their business processes. We have seen that managing risk in relation to vendors can be accomplished through due diligence, the selection process, contracting, and monitoring. Next we look at a proposed audit program for an outsourced function.

CHAPTER 6
AUDIT PROGRAM

An audit program for outsourcing cannot be generic since the process that underlies the outsourcing agreement is unique in every situation. What we present here is a general framework that would include audit steps for assessing most outsourcing relationships. The auditor would need to take into account the underlying process and add the appropriate audit steps for the given process. With that said, let us take a look at what a sample audit program might look like.

Planning the Audit — The first step in any successful audit is the planning stage. Planning sets the tone for the entire audit. During the planning stage, the auditor will establish the goals of the audit, document the purpose of the audit, and establish time lines, budgets, reporting formats, and a general description of the area under audit. Also, the auditor can identify reliance that can be placed on other controls or audits performed by other internal or external auditors.

Objectives — The objectives of the area that is being outsourced remain the same as they were when the process was being conducted in-house. What has changed at this point is the fact that you now have added another layer of objectives over the originals. The auditor is now faced with understanding the objectives of the outsourcing arrangement. Typically we have found that internal auditors are only auditing or becoming involved at a point after the contract has been signed and the process is in place. Through the survey, we were able to discern that most internal audit departments simply audit to the contract for compliance and report accordingly. We are arguing for complete involvement by internal audit from outsourcing inception to monitoring. We believe that a thorough audit should confirm management's assertions that outsourcing was not only necessary, but that it is economical, efficient, and effective.

The Team — The audit of outsourced services can require a specialized team in some instances. If the outsourced process is a complex and technical task, we recommend that the team members include:

- Subject matter expert from within the organization.
- An audit manager with experience in outsourcing.
- Staff auditor.

When auditing a complex outsourced process, you may run into great difficulty in gaining an understanding of the task. For this reason, we recommend using someone internally who has been assigned to this type of process before and is a subject matter expert in the area. The IIA's *Standards for the Professional Practice of Internal Auditing (Standards)* require that auditors should possess the knowledge, skills, and other competencies needed to perform their individual responsibilities. Also, the auditor needs to be aware that separate standards exist for the acceptance of consulting work. The auditor should only accept those engagements that have the potential to add value for the organization. If the process is too complex, we believe that an auditor would not have time to gain the knowledge necessary to perform the audit without the assistance of a subject matter expert.

Preliminary Review — Before the actual testing begins, the auditors need to complete some preliminary review procedures. For outsourcing, the auditors would:

- Set up an initial meeting with in-house personnel responsible for oversight.
- Set up an initial meeting with staff of vendor.

- Gain an understanding of the process through interviews and flowcharting.
  - Create a flowchart of outsourcing process to gain understanding (how did outsourcing decision start, what type of analysis was done, how was vendor selection completed, etc.).
- Gain an understanding of the outsourcing process by interviewing personnel responsible for outsourcing process and decision-making.
- Gather documents that relate to policies governing the outsourcing process (i.e., the actual due diligence documents for the outsourcing process/preliminary analysis worksheets, the contract, reports from vendor, etc.).
- Gather documents that relate to policies governing the work process itself (i.e., policies and procedures for the purchasing department).

Goals and Objectives of Audit

- Ensure that the outsourcing process complies with internal controls and policies.
- Ensure that due diligence occurred at each step of the process.
- Ensure that vendor selection process was adequate, impartial, and open.
- Ensure that contract negotiations include due diligence.
- Review contract for potential deficiencies or improvements.
- Verify that vendor's controls are functioning to meet goals of management.
- Ensure that vendor is substantially meeting the requirements of the contract.
- Verify that the work process (i.e., payroll) is functioning within internal control requirements to meet management's objectives.

Reliance on SAS 70 and Outside Auditors — In some instances, your vendor may be able to provide you with a SAS 70 report when you inquire about their internal control structure. Some service providers deal with so many clients and so many requests for internal control assurance that they engage outside independent audit firms to provide them with a report on their internal control structure. These reports are then given to clients whenever they ask for information about the vendors' ability to execute transactions. The reports help to assure the client that the vendor has the necessary controls in place to achieve managements' objectives. We believe that receiving SAS 70 reports are a part of due diligence and assurance. However, we also believe that this is only a small part of best practices and due diligence. As we have seen, outsourcing or strategic partnering creates new risks. The risks that are associated with outsourcing relate not only to the internal controls of your partner, but also to the entire process itself. Risks are created from the moment your organization considers outsourcing, and these additional risks must be addressed in conjunction with assuring internal control of the vendor.

Another disadvantage to relying on outsider auditors or SAS 70 reports is that they are typically generic in nature. They are based on guidelines developed by the AICPA and are well thought out and thorough, but in some instances they may not be tailored enough for your specific process. The internal auditor needs to be aware that the procurement and filing away of a SAS 70 or third-party audit does not constitute thorough due diligence. The internal audit staff must investigate and document that a SAS 70 report or any third-party report that makes assertions about the vendor's control environment is applicable to their unique situation. The internal audit staff should gather specific evidence about the vendor's controls that relate to the specific process that has been turned over.

Some have mentioned that they deal with vendors who cannot or do not provide SAS 70 reports. What can these organizations do to deal with the internal control risk? As we have mentioned, your organization needs to inquire during due diligence about the internal control structure of potential vendors. Vendors must be willing to make an assertion to you about their:

- Control environment.
- Risk assessment.
- Communication.
- Control activities.
- Monitoring.

If potential vendors are not willing to share and discuss these items with you or they are not willing to entertain a prospective audit by your staff, you should not engage them for outsourcing because you have no understanding of the true risk.

BEST PRACTICES ALERT

Through our research, roundtable, and questionnaire, we have developed a checklist of best practice guides for the outsourcing process. We believe, at a minimum, you should consider these issues when deciding to outsource:

Best Practices

- *Involve internal audit throughout the entire process.*
- *Gain an understanding of how and why the decision to outsource was made.*
- *Verify that alternatives were considered.*
- *Create a document that guides the process.*
- *Flowchart the process.*
- *Verify that a strategic analysis was done to ensure alignment with goals.*
- *Verify that a cost benefit analysis was done.*
- *Conduct a thorough risk assessment.*
- *Verify how the process will be overseen and by which personnel.*
- *Verify that a documented vendor selection process exists.*
- *Gain an understanding of vendor selection.*
- *Assess the risk of the vendor before selection.*
- *Create a unique, robust contract (see Chapter 4 for discussion).*
- *Monitor vendor and contract for compliance.*
- *Monitor the outsourcing process to ensure that it meets managements' objectives.*
- *Procure SAS 70 reports or outside audit reports when available.*
- *If no outside audit report is available, document the IC environment of the vendor.*

Next we look at a sample audit program: The phase in the outsourcing life cycle is shown in italics.

Control Objective	Risk	Audit Technique
Avoid interruption of Service *1. Analysis and Viability* *4. Monitoring*	Financial failure of vendor	Review of vendor financials. Completion of vendor ranking. Review of vendor contingency plan.
Ensure that relationship continues *3. Contract Negotiations*	Contract with vendor is flawed	Review contract for: Delineation of responsibilities. Measurable performance clause. Reasonable renewal periods. Outline of assets ownership. Outline of employees allocated. Use of blanket contract. Termination clause. Dispute resolution. Right to audit clause. Confidentiality agreement. Billing provisions.

Control Objective	Risk	Audit Technique
Ensure that outsourcing fits corporate strategy and meets objectives of company. *1. Analysis and Viability*	Outsourcing not aligned with corporate strategy.	Review company strategic plan. Review goals and objectives. Is process mission critical. Is process core competency.
Assure that only processes that are not critical are outsourced *1. Analysis and Viability*	Outsourced process is a core competency.	Review due diligence analysis. Gain understanding of process. Interview upper management.
Verify that vendor is completing transactions in a timely, effective and correct manner. *5. Monitoring*	Transactional risk	Tour vendor facilities. Observe process. Sample transactions for errors. Interview vendor management. Review vendor process documents. Review employees assigned. Review vendor contingency plan. Inspect for proper capacity.

Control Objective	Risk	Audit Technique
Ensure that vendor's actions do not cause loss of market position or goodwill. 5. *Monitoring*	Risk to reputation	Review process for illegal actions. Review for regulatory compliance. Review vendor credit report. Sample customers for comments. Review vendor financials.
Confirm that vendor is not engaged in illegal activities. 5. *Monitoring*	Legal risk	Review vendor's plan for compliance with legal and regulatory rules.
Ensure that risk of bringing process back in house has been addressed. 3. *Contract Negotiations*	Contract reversal risk	Review contract for language. Request document on plan for contract reversal. Review plan.
Ensure that competent staff are overseeing out-sourced process. 5. *Monitoring* 4. *Oversight*	Transactional risk	Interview management staff. Interview upper management. Confirm details of oversight process.

Control Objective	Risk	Audit Technique
Ensure that sound business reasons were used for decision to outsource. 1. *Analysis and Viability*	Business/ strategic risk	Determine where idea generated. Confirm need analysis was done. Confirm cost/ benefit analysis. Confirm alternatives considered.
Ensure that selection process included competitive bids and was impartial. 1. *Analysis and Viability* 2. *RFP and Proposal Review Stage*	Business/ strategic risk	Inspect RFPs. Review selection process. Review variables used for selection. Interview upper management.

CHAPTER 7
THE FUTURE

Technology is just one factor that has rapidly changed the way organizations have to operate to service customers and provide supply chain management. With the movement to even more e-business applications, most processes will require transactions through automated delivery channels. The audit group should have a thorough understanding on strategic alliances, vendor dependencies, and merger/acquisition situations that have impact on the performance of their goods and services. The strategic business plans of the organization should address not only the current vendors, but also those planned in the future. These factors are critical in setting the audit plan and resources.

The trend will be for increased reliance on vendors to provide non-core competencies so that organizations can focus on what they do best. With this trend it is more important that internal auditors step up to the demands of providing consulting and attestation services to meet the demands for corporations going forward. As organizations move to the virtual enterprise it will become even more difficult to define the line between components of an organization and those that support it. This blurring of boundaries makes it even more imperative that audit pay particular attention to those functions that were traditionally handled internally and not the typical "it's someone else's problem now."

As movement to the virtual corporation transpires, the role in vendor contracting and monitoring becomes even more important for functions like finance, audit, and legal. These functions become even more critical in the daily monitoring and compliance relationship for dealing with vendors. It becomes even more critical if the organization decides to outsource a function such as supply chain management and delegate responsibility for contracting vendor relationships. Internal audit then becomes a critical checkpoint if management is assuming too much risk by placing too much reliance on vendor performance.

For internal audit groups to be noted as providing best practice services in auditing vendor relationships in the future, they will have the following characteristics:

- Focus on risk mitigation models for vendor and partner selection.
- Integration of compliance tests dealing with key vendors as part of every audit.
- More focus on continuous monitoring of the operations, financial, and technology stability of critical vendors.
- Move from annual evaluation of vendors to monthly reviews, due to volatility of certain markets.
- Increased discussion among various audit and attest functions to collaborate on controls. Although auditors have not been entirely successful in this area in the past. Those who are successful will accomplish improved results by leveraging "trusted" relationships.
- Ensuring company focus on backup vendors and scenarios in case of vendor failure.
- Stronger ties with the supply chain management and understanding of those practices.
- Consulting services on the overall procurement practices.
- Increased attestation requests to ensure adequacy of vendor controls.
- Annual review of overall corporate policies and practices related to outsourcing.

We hope you all work toward best practices in dealing with your audit of vendor relationships while assisting your organizations in achieving success in managing the increased vendor relationships of the future. Internal audit has the opportunity to consult on the overall vendor control framework and provide assurance for operations of the future. As we have seen recently those companies and auditors not focused on the best practices of vendors may cause the organization to sustain significant losses or no longer be in business.

We strongly believe in The IIA motto "Progress Through Sharing," and those that live it will be living best practices of internal audit. We have included a number of case studies from practitioners in the Appendix as examples of sharing best practices.

APPENDIX A
CASE EXAMPLES

Provided by The IIA
www.theiia.org

However, the unavoidable reality is that when a company transfers a business operation to an outsource provider, it relinquishes control. *Regardless of how solid the motives for outsourcing are, the list of associated risks can be rather daunting, especially because once the process has been outsourced, the cost of bringing it back in-house is often staggering. In fact, most of the time, once the decision is made, it's practically irreversible. Failure to live up to the contracted agreement, lack of dedication or responsiveness, conflicting priorities, and service interruptions are all significant risks of outsourcing endeavors.*

To reduce some of these risks, many organizations solicit the aid of internal auditing to review outsourcing contracts before committing to a specific arrangement and to monitor the outsourcer throughout the duration of the relationship. Three internal auditors from organizations with successful outsourcing arrangements share their best practices and tips for taking the worry out of hiring a third-party provider.

FULFILLMENT

Jean Moyer
Vice President & Director of Internal Audit
National Geographic Society

Because of the large amount of outsourcing contracted by National Geographic Society, our internal audit group spends 60 percent of the year auditing outside the company. The most significant function we outsource is fulfillment, which used to be performed in-house by approximately 800 staff members. The function consists of fulfilling a customer's subscription or book order, getting the product to the customer, and collecting money. For us, this process is critical because we offer four magazines, a large book line, educational products, and catalog products.

The greatest risks we face from contracting with a third-party provider include damage to our company's reputation due to customer service problems and improper handling of our business. When members, subscribers, or purchasers of our products call our customer service number, they think they're talking to someone who works for National Geographic, because that's how the phone is answered by our vendor. Therefore, the customer service representatives have to be trained well to handle difficult situations tactfully.

To monitor outsourcing arrangements for these and any other potential problems, National Geographic has in-house business units solely devoted to managing outsource vendors. These groups, which aren't part of internal auditing, oversee the company's relationship with the various outsource vendors that provide our fulfillment services. For example, customer service telephone conversations are taped for quality assurance, and business division members listen to the tapes to determine if the representatives are being rude or answering questions incorrectly.

When our internal auditors plan an audit of an outsource vendor, we always go through the in-house group and determine whether there have been any concerns or unexpected situations throughout the year that may have affected the controls in place. That helps us highlight the critical areas and risks upon which we base our audit plans. Additionally, the group often sends one staff member with us toward the end of the audit to review the findings with the outsource vendor, which is beneficial because it demonstrates a united front from our company.

We also perform information technology audits at the outsource vendors' locations. Our technology auditor talks with the vendor's technology staff and determines whether they have adequate security, password control, change control, and disaster and backup recovery. The interaction provides assurance that our data sitting on their systems is well controlled. Adequate controls are particularly important, because our outsource vendors deal with phone orders and customers' credit card numbers. We need to ensure that confidential information is not readily accessible and that changes cannot intentionally be made to corrupt the data.

Ultimately, auditing should get in on the relationship with the outsource vendor as early as possible — preferably before the contract is signed — and ensure that the contract not only includes a right-to-audit clause, but also allows practitioners to audit beyond the financial records. If the relationship is established early, it's much easier.

REVENUE PROCESSING

Dave Richards
Chief Audit Executive
FirstEnergy Corp.

FirstEnergy Corp., an energy supplier with more than 2 million customers in Ohio and Pennsylvania, used to outsource a portion of its revenue-processing function. A third-party provider collected customer payments, processed and deposited the cash receipts, and sent the compiled payment information to FirstEnergy for entry into the company's accounts receivable system. Revenue processing is a risky process to outsource, because errors or processing delays can substantially affect other company operations.

One of the most critical ways that internal auditing helps mitigate outsourcing risks is by getting involved before the decision to outsource is even made. For the past five to six years, we've concentrated our efforts on participating in up-front analysis and the decision-making process to help our clients examine their reasons for wanting to outsource, determine if hiring a third-party provider is appropriate, and determine what they can expect from the arrangement.

Internal auditing is ideal for providing this type of assistance because we have the necessary analytical, communication, documentation, and business skills. We also have networks across organizational boundaries, enabling us to know the people and processes within the company, especially how they affect other operations.

When determining whether to outsource, it's critical that process owners consider the other areas of the business that may be affected by the success of their business process. The decision can't be made in a vacuum. If outsourcing is found to be appropriate, auditing works with our internal operations to ensure that the right structure, provider, and contract are selected.

If the decision to outsource has already been made before auditing gets involved, then it's important for auditing to work with the relationship manager, the internal person responsible for overseeing the efficiency and effectiveness of the third-party provider. An appropriate relationship manager must be identified and trained to maximize the relationship to the benefit of both parties. The biggest mistake companies make is that they try to take the person who was in charge of the function when it was done internally and make him or her the relationship manager. However, relationship managers require a separate set of skills for relationship building, performance measurement, process involvement, contract administration, and building internal trust. They should constantly think about future developments that could impact others in the business and ways to push the outsource provider to be innovative.

When it's time to audit the third-party provider, our auditors work with the customers — the internal people responsible for the outsourced operation — and conduct facilitated work sessions to help identify relevant risks. Then, we perform risk mapping and control assessment to determine the risks' impact on operations and overall cost. Ultimately, we focus the audit on the high-risk, high-probability items, particularly those with inadequate controls.

MEDICAL CLAIMS

Tom Mock
Director of Internal Audit
Hughes Supply

Hughes Supply, a multi-branch wholesale distributor of plumbing, water and sewer, electrical, and industrial products, is a self-insured company. Rather than signing up with an independent medical insurance provider, the company pays medical claims out of its own checking account. However, Hughes has outsourced this function, hiring a third-party provider to oversee the processing of medical claims. When an employee visits a physician, for example, the claim is submitted to the outsource provider for processing, and the provider issues payment to the physician. To ensure that the medical claims checking account is properly funded, Hughes deposits money into the account based on financial statements of medical claims processed by the outsource vendor weekly.

In this case, the risk of the outsource vendor providing inadequate service can be rather costly. Therefore, one of the most critical steps our audit group can take to protect the company is to audit the actual contract agreement with the third-party provider. **Surprisingly, we've found that most vendors have never had someone perform an audit of their standard agreement.**

Another successful strategy we've adopted is to provide specialized training to auditors prior to assigning them to audit a technical area. For example, every year prior to auditing our health care claims provider, auditors are sent to a health care conference or seminar. The audit team is encouraged to talk to the people at the conference, especially the speakers, because they frequently have insight into high-risk areas and issues that auditors should investigate.

Our audit group has found it crucial to maintain open communication with the vendors as well as the internal departments responsible for administrating the terms of the contract. We believe that the best way to begin an audit is to meet with the internal department manager who has responsibility for daily administration of the outsourced service. We discuss the positive aspects of the vendor's service as well as some of the daily issues. Next, we hold a meeting with both the manager and the vendor's key personnel to discuss expectations such as the scope and time of the audit, resource requirements, and deliverables. We also solicit their feedback and ask if there's any information they would like us to provide. In the end, this approach creates a win-win situation where we benefit from the nonthreatening relationship, and the vendor gains valuable information about the company and learns ways to improve controls and reduce cost.

JOINT BENEFITS

The risks of hiring an outsource vendor may vary depending on the location and complexity of the provider, vendor cooperation, accessibility to data, timing and resource constraints, and management's support. However, regardless of the seemingly endless challenges that outsourcing arrangements pose, internal auditors can make all the difference in whether the engagement is successful. When auditors operate in a proactive, value-added manner, they may discover that the vendors not only welcome the audit, but take advantage of it to learn about their clients and improve their services. Some providers may even view the audit as free consulting.

APPENDIX B
SURVEY RESULTS

In preparation of this Handbook the authors designed a survey that would provide additional insight in the area of vendor management. We would especially like to thank everyone who completed the survey and provided valuable information in this area.

The survey was made available on The IIA GAIN site and a summary of the survey results is included below. We have also included our interruptive comments of the results. We had 165 responses to the survey of those responding all had internal audit departments.

1. The question below dealt with what areas are outsourced. We found a wide diversity of functions that are outsourced, with information technology being the area most commonly outsourced. Those that were highly outsourced were in the areas of capital and resource intensive or areas requiring technical expertise.

1. What areas of your business are 100% outsourced?

Choice	Count	Percent of Sample
Other, please indicate:	42	25.3%
Information Technology (help desk, data center)	38	22.9%
Employee Benefits	25	15.1%
Facilities Management/Maintenance	23	13.9%
Payroll	20	12.0%
Legal	17	10.2%

Choice	Count	Percent of Sample
Customer Service/Call Center	10	6.0%
Manufacturing	5	3.0%
Purchasing	3	1.8%
Financial	2	1.2%
Human Resources	2	1.2%
Accounting	1	0.6%
Supply Chain Management	1	0.6%

2. A number of questions dealt with the degree of internal audit involvement in the early stages to outsource. A very high percentage (72%) were not involved in the decision to outsource. However, 83.4% felt audit should be involved in the due diligence phase of outsourcing.

2. Does the internal audit department get involved with the decision-making process for the creation of an outsourcing partnership?

Choice	Count	Percentage Answered
Yes	46	28.0%
No	118	72.0%

3. Similar to the results on other IIA surveys and belief of audit involvement in the front-end review of the control infrastructure, a high percentage of auditors believe that internal audit should be involved in outsourced operations.

   3. Do you believe internal audit should be involved in the due diligence of outsourced operations?

Choice	Count	Percentage Answered
Yes	136	83.4%
No	27	16.6%

4. The area that internal audit is typically most involved in is the traditional review and monitoring of vendor activities with 57.8%.

   4. What role does internal audit play in creating an outsourcing relationship?

Choice	Count	Percent of Sample
Review and audit of vendor activities	96	57.8%
Vendor criteria requirements	35	21.1%
Outsource cost/benefit analysis	24	14.5%
Implementation and integration of vendor into process	20	12.0%
Selection of vendor	14	8.4%
Decision to outsource	8	4.8%

5. Management is the primary driver with a combined total of 95.3% of the response that management generated the decision to outsource.

5. The decision to outsource was generated at what level?

Choice	Count	Percent of Sample
Top management	117	70.5%
Middle level management	42	25.3%
Supervisory	2	1.2%
Staff	1	0.6%
Vendor generated and initiated	4	2.4%

6. From the responses on the next question, many areas are considered when outsourcing, which may be part of the reason why outsourcing contracts take a lot of time to put in place. The most significant of those factors being considered being in the areas of quality and financial. From the other answers given by respondents it should be noted that contract considerations seem to be customized to the particular outsourcing arrangement and the control environment of the company.

6. What business decisions were considered when deciding to outsource?

Choice	Count	Percent of Sample
Quality assurance	90	54.2%
Financial standards for vendor	84	50.6%
Confidentiality	78	47.0%
Term of relationship	74	44.6%
Personnel	72	43.4%
Security	66	39.8%

Asset Ownership/License	62	37.3%
Agreements/Insurance		
Regulatory Compliance	61	36.7%
Division of Responsibilities	59	35.5%
Disputes/Terminations	57	34.3%
Billing Provisions	56	33.7%
Additional Services	50	30.1%

7. The two most important audit factors to be included in the decision to outsource included providing audit access to information and vendor's agreement to adhere to regulatory concerns. From the comments received it should be noted that audit considerations are not a driving decision in outsourcing, but typically are addressed after the decision is made to outsource.

7. What audit factors are typically considered when deciding to outsource?

Choice	Count	Percent of Sample
Will vendor provide access to all information?	79	47.6%
Is it agreed that vendor will adhere to regulatory concerns?	68	41.0%
Is vendor required to respond to all audit matters?	64	38.6%
Is scheduling of audits agreed upon?	46	27.7%
Has consideration been given to working with external auditors?	31	18.7%
Will vendor provide assistance at no charge?	29	17.5%
Is there a relationship with regulators?	25	15.1%

Choice	Count	Percent of Sample
Is there a process in place for distribution of audit reports?	22	13.3%
Will vendor limit number of auditors?	21	12.7%
Will vendor provide work space at no charge?	14	8.4%

8. Although 43.3% of the responses showed internal audit groups having an audit program in place for addressing vendor relationships, only 38.8% of the audit groups perform systematic audits of outsourced vendors.

8. Does the internal audit department have an audit program in place for vendor relationships?

Choice	Count	Percentage Answered
Yes	71	43.3%
No	90	54.9%
Don't know	3	1.8%
Don't have audit group	0	0.0%

9. As noted from some of the responses, many of the audit groups don't have the necessary resources to perform reviews of vendors or rely on management controls over vendors. Another approach that seems to be successful with limited resources is to leverage the responsibility of a control review to a vendor auditor of the vendor or third-party auditor. The authors believe a risk-based approach to review of those vendors of extremely high risk should be performed; however, reliance on "trusted" auditor may also suffice.

9. Does internal audit perform a systematic review of outsourced vendors?

Choice	Count	Percentage Answered
Yes	64	38.8%
No	97	58.8%
Not audited	4	2.4%

10. Another control measure is for audit to document and review compliance to the contract. Since it is much easier to audit what has been contracted than to make contract revisions, a number of audit groups take this approach. A key element of this is an understanding of the design of the control environment.

10. Is it normal practice for the internal audit department to confirm and document the controls that the vendor has put in place to ensure contract compliance?

Choice	Count	Percentage Answered
Yes	65	40.4%
No	96	59.6%

11. A risk assessment of the vendor control environment is one area
    that audit can assist management. This is one area where 57.5%
    of the audit groups responded that risk evaluation is one area of
    involvement in the outsource agreement.

   **11. Is it normal practice for the internal audit department
   to identify and document the risks associated with the
   outsourced service?**

Choice	Count	Percentage Answered
Yes	92	57.5%
No	68	42.5%

12. Similar to previous responses, internal audit many times ensures
    the ongoing contract and service-level agreement are in place.

   **12. Is it normal practice for the internal audit department
   to verify and document the existence of a service-level
   agreement with performance monitoring procedures?**

Choice	Count	Percentage Answered
Yes	87	54.4%
No	63	39.4%
Unsure	10	6.3%

We had a number of free form comments on the survey and have summarized those below:

The other areas outsourced include the following: food services (5), university bookstore (2), copy operations (2), proprietary credit cards (3), accounts receivable, tourism promotion, fixed deposits received from the public, accounts payable, building security and maintenance, internal mail distribution, workers' compensation reporting, maintenance and health care reporting and operations, risk management, construction activities, fulfillment services, workers' compensation, auto liability claims, general insurance claims, fire rescue fee billing and collection, indigent health care payment process, printing benefit checks and explanation of benefits, scanning claims, e-mail, other numerous industry-specific operational tasks, outsourced contract labor, relocation services, IT services, freight payment processing, and data entry.

Other comments that were made included the following:

- Audit should also ensure that decision to outsource was not taken only with a view to avoid consolidating assets or activities (ad hoc entities).

- We have performed audits such as an audit of vendor access to our facilities. Contracts and the monitoring of contracts is management's responsibility. In our company, our role is to monitor high-risk contracts to ensure compliance with their provisions.

- We do not outsource or plan to outsource any core activity.

- While audit is not generally involved in the decision of who the outsourcer will be (and selection criteria), audit is asked for input on the "audit ability" of a vendor (from audit clause up to whether the contract, as written, can be audited against.

- Audit's role is to ensure management has appropriate monitoring controls in place over the outsourced operations, such controls include a designated and accountable contract manager, formal service-level agreements with quantitative measures, regular review and validation of vendor performance and statistics to support billings and/or receipt of incentives or application of penalties per contract terms.

- Outsourcing is generally engaged when we are looking for subject matter experts with a clear deliverable typically with a fixed fee arrangement.

- I believe that corporations should have policies regarding who should be involved in outsource decisions — audit, legal, finance, — as well as the operating areas.

- We also rely heavily on SAS 70 reports.

- There should always be an audit clause in outsourcing agreements. Auditors should be involved as early as possible in the process. Audits should be performed in every case no matter how good the relationship might be.

- Although IA is involved in the process to review a decision to outsource to a vendor, rarely does the right to audit get addressed explicitly enough in the contract to allow for an efficient audit. (i.e., timing, access to documents, who pays, etc.). All this gets discussed after the contract is signed and when the negotiations are performed and much more difficult.

- For financial institutions, many on the considerations noted above are outlined in detailed regulatory guidance on this subject. The regulatory authorities look for these practices during their routine examinations. In some instances, the regulators are to be informed when outsourcing decisions are made. In many cases, vendors' SAS 70 reports are the primary source of information and they are specifically requested as part of the due diligence and subsequent ongoing review process.

- There is a growing awareness among top managers that audit arrangements (including access to information and personnel) with service providers should have been given greater attention.

- The only audit we regularly perform of an outsourced function was recommended by the regulator. Otherwise, usually performed following management request.

- We receive copies of audit reports from the vendor's auditors and, to a great extent, place reliance on their work.

- My department is staffed with two people so to call anything Normal is difficult. I consider outsourcing when performing my annual risk assessment. Outsourcing is a problem with my company. It seems that we tend to outsource in an attempt to lessen management responsibilities without regard for the new risks from outsourcing, which has caused us problems in the past. I've voiced my concern over this practice. Internal audit does and has audited outsourced arrangements, post implementation. Given my department's size, I've pushed and obtained the development of a comprehensive procurement policy. It's my goal to have our procurement group oversee the outsourcing procedures rather than internal audit. To me the bigger risk is when a department decides to outsource, does not use skilled procurement professionals, and thinks they have the necessary skills. Procurement professionals bring objectivity and procedures to the process and are a buffer between the outsourcer and the department. If a strong procurement function exists, then at a minimum internal audit should be involved in consulting with procurement on procurement controls and audit concerns. However, I have been involved in large outsourcing projects, which large sums of money were saved due to our involvement. If internal audit department is large enough, then I recommend their proactive involvement. The first line of control should be involvement of skilled procurement professionals.

- Although internal auditing was included in the activities and processes covered, it was not in a decision-making capacity.

- We have very little outsourced services. As such, this does not come up very often, but the areas suggested to be looked at from an audit perspective make sense.

- Each contract has unique audit requirements.

- As a public educational institution, we really do not have any outsourced functions.

- The company has 88,000 vendors. It would not be feasible for the internal audit department to audit all vendors on a regular basis.

- Only vendors that we generally outsource are for information systems development and implementation. We follow the standard SDLC process for selecting and monitoring these contractors.

- We do very little outsourcing. We have employed implementation partners to assist in implementing new software applications. Our audit department is very small (two people) for an organization with over 4,000 employees. Audit has little time to devote to outsourcing issues.

- Outsourcing occurs in many lines of business and for different reasons. Audit's role is to be involved but not to decide or to actually implement. We want to make sure that there are processes in place that will lead to the correct decision and management of these firms. We do development work, which includes vendor selection as well as on-site post conversion work, and also vendor management audits. We partner with the line of business to do the on-site work. Business units are also responsible for risk and control analysis, which general auditing will audit as part of its development audit work. Our audit approach is risk-based and therefore our coverage of OSPs and vendor management will be likewise.

- Outsourcing decisions have been primarily the responsibility of the operations department to administer as part of their overall departmental goals and objectives. In other words, there are certain profit margins that they are expected to achieve; if outsourcing will help achieve those margins, the outsourcing decision is made by the individual departmental or manufacturing organizational head responsible for the "operating results."

- Normal practice to conduct such reviews AFTER function is outsourced.

- Internal audit has typically not been involved in vendor audits, other than the audit of payments made to these vendors as part of an overall accounts payable audit activities.

- Management is solely responsible for managing the outsourced relationship. Internal audit has provided a Service Provider Due Diligence Program and assists in its completion upon request.

- Audit factors were not considered in deciding to outsource.

The following questions are the responses related to the demographics of those answering the survey:

Q.B1 Country:

Item	Frequency	Percent
USA	135	81.3%
CAN	8	4.8%
GBR	7	4.2%
PHL	2	1.2%
FRA, PRI, BRA, PRT, FIN, AUS, IND, ZAF, IRL, POL, MEX, LBN, GRC, THA	14	8.4%
Total	166	100.0%

Sample Answering: 166 responses

Q.B2 Industry

Item	Frequency	Percent
Educational Institutions	24	14.5%
Health Care	10	6.0%
Services	4	2.4%
Manufacturing	23	13.9%
Banking, Financial	26	15.7%
Chemical, Drug	8	4.8%
Utilities	15	9.0%
Wholesale, Retail	8	4.8%
Communications	5	3.0%
Petroleum	6	3.6%
Computer Technology	3	1.8%
Insurance	11	6.6%
Agriculture, Mining or Construction	4	2.4%
Transportation	8	4.8%
Government	9	5.4%
(Unique responses)	2	1.2%
(Total)	166	100.0%

Sample Answering: 166 responses

B3 - Annual revenue (government and banks use asset size):

Choice	Count	Percentage Answered
Under $100 million	9	5.4%
$100 million to $500 million	37	22.3%
$500 million to $1 billion	25	15.1%
$1 billion to $5 billion	55	33.1%
$5 billion to $10 billion	17	10.2%
$10 billion to $30 billion	12	7.2%
Over $30 billion	11	6.6%

B4 - Number of full-time employees:

Choice	Count	Percentage Answered
Under 500	13	7.9%
500 to 1,000	14	8.5%
1,000 to 5,000	61	37.0%
5,000 to 10,000	26	15.8%
10,000 to 25,000	26	15.8%
25,000 to 50,000	11	6.7%
Over 50,000	14	8.5%

B5 - Are you a member of The Institute of Internal Auditors?

Choice	Count	Percentage Answered
Yes	153	92.2%
No	13	7.8%